Questions for Couples Journal with Prompts

365 Questions for Couples to Connect and Spark Meaningful Conversations with Your Partner

NICOLE JONES

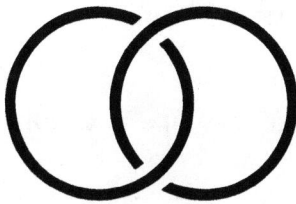

Contents

Introduction

Ever heard of 21 questions? Well, how about a question for each day of the year?

We, humans, are so multifaceted, and there are so many little intricacies and nooks and crannies in our personalities and what makes each of us our unique selves, that getting to know someone is a never-ending journey! Often, there are things we don't know about one another, not because we're hiding anything or keeping secrets, but simply because we've never asked. We've never thought to ask.

Playing question games is a very simple, fun, and connective way to get to know those around you a little better, especially when it comes to our romantic relationships. We can continue learning about one another for the rest of our lives if we wish to. Quite often, however, we stop being curious. We think we know someone as well as we can, and then we accept them as we think we know them to be, and we go about life with this acceptance. What happens when we commit to continuing the exploration of our partners? What happens when we recognize that, just like ourselves, our partners are continuously evolving and changing through the seasons of their lives, and therefore our relationship is really a space for continuous re-acquainting with one another?

Through this book, there are 365 questions offered for couples to consider as they endeavor to continue exploring one another. Use them as you wish: all at once, one per day, section by section - it's really up to you. Consider each carefully, answer honestly, and see how well you can get to know your loved one. You may be surprised by what comes up in your journey together!

Questions
of The Past

HOW DID YOU BECOME YOU?

1. What is your first memory/the first thing you can remember?

_____

_____

_____

_____

_____

_____

_____

_____

2. Who do you remember being around the most as a child?

_____

_____

_____

_____

_____

_____

_____

_____

3. What was your favorite color as a child?

_____

_____

_____

_____

_____

_____

_____

4. What was your favorite place to be as a child?

_____

_____

_____

_____

_____

_____

_____

5. What did your bedroom look like as a child?

_____

_____

_____

_____

_____

_____

_____

6. Where did you live?

_____

_____

_____

_____

_____

_____

_____

7. Who did you live with?

_____

_____

_____

_____

_____

_____

_____

_____

8. If you had to describe your childhood in one word, what would it be?

_____

_____

_____

_____

_____

_____

_____

_____

9. Who was your childhood best friend? Tell me about them! What would you two do together?

_____

_____

_____

_____

_____

_____

_____

_____

10. Were you an outdoorsy child? Or did you prefer to be inside?

_____

_____

_____

_____

_____

_____

_____

_____

11. Did you enjoy school?

_____

_____

_____

_____

_____

_____

_____

_____

12. What was your favorite subject in school?

_____

_____

_____

_____

_____

_____

_____

_____

13. What did you want to be when you grew up?

_____

_____

_____

_____

_____

_____

_____

_____

14. Were you extroverted or introverted as a child?

_____

_____

_____

_____

_____

_____

_____

_____

15. What were the rules of your household?

_____

_____

_____

_____

_____

_____

_____

_____

16. Are there any foods you remember strongly from your childhood?

_____

_____

_____

_____

_____

_____

_____

_____

17. What was your favorite food growing up?

_____

_____

_____

_____

_____

_____

_____

_____

18. Do you have any siblings? If so, were you close growing up? What was your relationship with them like?

_____

_____

_____

_____

_____

_____

_____

_____

19. What was your relationship with your parents or guardians like as a child?

_____

_____

_____

_____

_____

_____

_____

_____

20. What were you like as a teenager?

_____

_____

_____

_____

_____

_____

_____

_____

21. What type of music did 'the teenage' you listen to?

_____

_____

_____

_____

_____

_____

_____

22. Who was your celebrity crush as a teen?

_____

_____

_____

_____

_____

_____

_____

23. Were you curious about sexuality as a teen?

_____

_____

_____

_____

_____

_____

_____

_____

24. What was your friendship group like as a teen?

_____

_____

_____

_____

_____

_____

_____

_____

25. What did your bedroom look like as a teen?

_____

_____

_____

_____

_____

_____

_____

_____

26. Did you like high school?

_____

_____

_____

_____

_____

_____

_____

_____

27. Did you have any hobbies/special interests?

_____

_____

_____

_____

_____

_____

_____

28. What did you think you were going to be when you grew up?

_____

_____

_____

_____

_____

_____

_____

29. Did you have any pets growing up? If more than one, tell me about all of them. Which was your favorite? If you never had a pet, was there one you always wanted?

_____

_____

_____

_____

_____

_____

_____.

30. What was your relationship with your parents or guardians like as a teenager?

_____

_____

_____

_____

_____

_____

_____.

31. Did you have grandparents around? What were they like?

_____

_____

_____

_____

_____

_____

_____

32. Did you have a large family or a small family?

_____

_____

_____

_____

_____

_____

_____

33. What were holidays/occasions like in your family?

_____

_____

_____

_____

_____

_____

_____

_____.

34. Who was your role model growing up?

_____

_____

_____

_____

_____

_____

_____

_____.

35. Did you aspire to continue your education after high school, or were you more excited for school to be a thing of the past?

_____

_____

_____

_____

_____

_____

_____

_____

36. What is the first profession you wanted to have as a child?

_____

_____

_____

_____

_____

_____

_____

_____

37. What was your transition into early adulthood like?

_____

_____

_____

_____

_____

_____

_____

38. What was the most challenging part of early adulthood for you?

_____

_____

_____

_____

_____

_____

_____

39. When did you move out of your family home, if ever?

_____

_____

_____

_____

_____

_____

_____

_____

40. When did you lose your virginity? What was this experience like?

_____

_____

_____

_____

_____

_____

_____

_____

41. Tell me about your first love.

_____

_____

_____

_____

_____

_____

_____

_____

42. Tell me about your first real heartbreak.

_____

_____

_____

_____

_____

_____

_____

_____

43. If you could give your younger self one piece of advice, what would it be?

_____

_____

_____

_____

_____

_____

_____

_____

_____

_____

_____

_____

_____

_____

_____

Past Lives

WHO HAVE YOU BEEN?

44. What was the best thing you learned from your parents or guardians?

_____

_____

_____

_____

_____

_____

_____

_____

45. Are there any specific skills you learned from your mother or another female role model? Your father or another male role model? Another family member?

_____

_____

_____

_____

_____

_____

_____

_____

46. What were you proud of as a child?

_____

_____

_____

_____

_____

_____

_____

_____

47. What was your first job?

_____

_____

_____

_____

_____

_____

_____

_____

48. What was your favorite job you ever had?

_____

_____

_____

_____

_____

_____

_____

49. Can you list all the jobs you've ever had, in chronological order?

_____

_____

_____

_____

_____

_____

_____

50. What are your top five most random skills?

_____

_____

_____

_____

_____

_____

_____

51. How has your identity changed over the years?

_____

_____

_____

_____

_____

_____

_____

52. Is there any piece of your identity that has always stayed the same?

_____

_____

_____

_____

_____

_____

_____

_____.

53. Have you ever had a "Tower" moment? Referring to The Tower card in tarot, when everything feels like it's crumbling, and you have to start from scratch?

_____

_____

_____

_____

_____

_____

_____

_____.

54. Tell me about your first romantic relationship. This doesn't have to be your first love, but your first time experiencing a romantic relationship and the feelings that go along with it. What was your biggest learning from this relationship?

_____

_____

_____

_____

_____

_____

_____

_____

55. How many long-term romantic relationships have you had?

_____

_____

_____

_____

_____

_____

_____

_____

56. Which relationship do you feel changed/affected you the most?

_____

_____

_____

_____

_____

_____

_____

_____

57. Have you ever really changed for someone else? Tell me about it.

_____

_____

_____

_____

_____

_____

_____

_____

58. How has your sexuality changed over time?

_____

_____

_____

_____

_____

_____

_____

_____.

59. Has your relationship concerning gender and gender expression changed over time? How or how not?

_____

_____

_____

_____

_____

_____

_____

_____.

60. Is there anything you've ever felt particularly ashamed about?

_____

_____

_____

_____

_____

_____

_____

_____

61. Where do you feel most at home? What about this place feels like home to you?

_____

_____

_____

_____

_____

_____

_____

_____

62. Can you list all the places you've lived, in chronological order?

_____

_____

_____

_____

_____

_____

_____

_____

63. Of all the places you've lived, which was your favorite?

_____

_____

_____

_____

_____

_____

_____

_____

64. Can you recall your first time traveling, whether it be to another country or just another region? Who did you go with? Where did you go? What did you do? What was the experience like?

_____

_____

_____

_____

_____

_____

_____

_____

65. Can you list all the places you've ever traveled, in chronological order?

_____

_____

_____

_____

_____

_____

_____

_____

66. How has your personal style changed over time, regarding fashion or simply how you like to present yourself to the world?

_____

_____

_____

_____

_____

_____

_____

_____.

67. What was your most dramatic style phase? Was there a time when you were very committed to portraying a certain image? Did you go full punk mode, or full perm at any point in your life?

_____

_____

_____

_____

_____

_____

_____

_____.

68. Is there a particular item of clothing you have that recalls a specific time in your life? Or one you remember?

_____

_____

_____

_____

_____

_____

_____

_____

69. Do you have any items of clothing that are particularly sentimental? Why?

_____

_____

_____

_____

_____

_____

_____

70. When you think of your childhood self, what clothing item comes to mind?

_____

_____

_____

_____

_____

_____

_____

71. When you think of your teenage self, what clothing item comes to mind?

_____

_____

_____

_____

_____

_____

_____

72. When you think of your young adult self, what clothing item comes to mind?

_____

_____

_____

_____

_____

_____

_____

_____.

73. Did you ever have - or do you have - any tattoos or piercings?

_____

_____

_____

_____

_____

_____

_____

_____.

74. If you have tattoos and piercings, what was your first? If not, would you ever get one? Where would you get it and what would it be?

_____

_____

_____

_____

_____

_____

_____

_____

75. Did you go through a rebellious phase? How did you rebel? What were you rebelling against?

_____

_____

_____

_____

_____

_____

_____

_____

76. In your past, how would your friends describe you?

_____

_____

_____

_____

_____

_____

_____

77. In your past, how would your co-workers describe you?

_____

_____

_____

_____

_____

_____

_____

78. In your past, how would your family describe you?

_____

_____

_____

_____

_____

_____

_____

_____

79. In your past, how would any previous partners describe you?

_____

_____

_____

_____

_____

_____

_____

_____

80. In your past, how would you have described yourself?

_____

_____

_____

_____

_____

_____

_____

_____

81. If you had to describe yourself as a teenager or young person in three words, what would they be?

_____

_____

_____

_____

_____

_____

_____

_____

Questions of The Present

WHO ARE YOU NOW?

82. Do you know the history of your family name? For example, the culture it originates from or if it has any meaning to it?

_____

_____

_____

_____

_____

_____

_____.

83. Do you like your given name?

_____

_____

_____

_____

_____

_____

_____.

84. Does your name have any sentimental, cultural, symbolic, or other, meaning?

_____

_____

_____

_____

_____

_____

_____

_____

85. Were you named after someone? How was your name chosen?

_____

_____

_____

_____

_____

_____

_____

_____

86. What name did you love as a child? Perhaps of a classmate, family member, or even a celebrity.

_____

_____

_____

_____

_____

_____

_____

_____

87. Did you have any nicknames growing up?

_____

_____

_____

_____

_____

_____

_____

_____

88. Do you have any nicknames now?

_____

_____

_____

_____

_____

_____

_____

_____

89. How do you feel about nicknames, whether receiving them, giving them to others, or using them toward others? Do you love them, find they give a sense of comradery, or do you hate them?

_____

_____

_____

_____

_____

_____

_____

_____

90. Have you ever thought about changing your name? If you could choose your name, different from the one your parents gave you, what would it be?

_____

_____

_____

_____

_____

_____

_____

_____.

91. Do you consider yourself spiritual? What does this mean to you?

_____

_____

_____

_____

_____

_____

_____

_____.

92. What is your relationship with religion like? Did you grow up in a religious household? How has your relationship with religion changed over time?

_____

_____

_____

_____

_____

_____

_____

93. What is your most masculine and feminine attribute? Do you feel more connected to one or the other, or feel both within you? Do you notice a tendency to reject one or the other in yourself? How do you express masculinity or femininity?

_____

_____

_____

_____

_____

_____

_____

94. Do you feel that you present authentically to the world? Is the way you feel on the inside the way you present yourself to the world?

_____

_____

_____

_____

_____

_____

_____

_____

95. What is your dream job? Are you currently in your dream job? How would you change your job to better satisfy you?

_____

_____

_____

_____

_____

_____

_____

_____

96. What is the best part of your day, each day?

_____

_____

_____

_____

_____

_____

_____

_____

97. Do you feel like you've grown in the past year? Why, or why not?

_____

_____

_____

_____

_____

_____

_____

_____

98. What are you proud of?

_____

_____

_____

_____

_____

_____

_____

_____

99. Do you carry any regrets?

_____

_____

_____

_____

_____

_____

_____

_____

100. What are your closest relationships in life?

_____

_____

_____

_____

_____

_____

_____

101. What is your favorite characteristic that you have?

_____

_____

_____

_____

_____

_____

_____

102. What are you exceptionally good at?

_____

_____

_____

_____

_____

_____

_____

103. What are you terrible at?

_____

_____

_____

_____

_____

_____

_____

104. What do you wish to get better at?

_____

_____

_____

_____

_____

_____

_____.

105. Are there any skills you'd like to learn?

_____

_____

_____

_____

_____

_____

_____.

106. Where has your mind been wandering off to recently?

_____

_____

_____

_____

_____

_____

_____

_____

107. If you could cancel all your obligations and completely clear your schedule for next week to do whatever you want in the world, how would you spend your week?

_____

_____

_____

_____

_____

_____

_____

_____

108. What is your favorite way to spend an evening, and why?

_____

_____

_____

_____

_____

_____

_____.

109. What is your favorite time of day, and why?

_____

_____

_____

_____

_____

_____

_____.

110. What is your favorite season, and why?

_____

_____

_____

_____

_____

_____

_____

_____

111. What is your favorite month, and why?

_____

_____

_____

_____

_____

_____

_____

_____

112. Do you feel you get enough sleep? When you wake up in the morning, do you usually feel fully rested or like you could sleep for another six hours?

_____

_____

_____

_____

_____

_____

_____

_____

113. Do you have any bizarre sleeping habits? Any silly sleeping positions? Do you drool? Do you talk in your sleep?

_____

_____

_____

_____

_____

_____

_____

_____

114. Are you ticklish? If so, where?

_____

_____

_____

_____

_____

_____

_____

_____

115. What was the last dream you remember having? Do you have any memories of specifically vivid or impactful dreams?

_____

_____

_____

_____

_____

_____

_____

_____

116. Has there been anything specific coming up in your dreams recently or any repetitive dreams you've ever had?

_____

_____

_____

_____

_____

_____

_____

_____

_____

117. Do you like where you live?

_____

_____

_____

_____

_____

_____

_____

_____

118. If you could live anywhere in the world, where would you live?

_____

_____

_____

_____

_____

_____

_____

119. Why don't you live there now?

_____

_____

_____

_____

_____

_____

_____

120. What do you fear the most?

_____

_____

_____

_____

_____

_____

_____

_____.

121. If you had to describe/categorize this time in your life in one word, what would it be?

_____

_____

_____

_____

_____

_____

_____

_____.

Ogres Are Like Onions

LAYERS OF BEING

122. Do you feel you are good at being open about your emotions or do you tend to keep things inside?

_____

_____

_____

_____

_____

_____

_____

_____

123. Do you often feel like you're being honest about how you're feeling?

_____

_____

_____

_____

_____

_____

_____

_____

124. Do you find it challenging to express yourself?

_____

_____

_____

_____

_____

_____

_____

125. Is/are there any part(s) of you that you've never shared with anyone else?

_____

_____

_____

_____

_____

_____

_____

126. What is your biggest secret?

_____

_____

_____

_____

_____

_____

_____

127. Do you consider yourself secretive?

_____

_____

_____

_____

_____

_____

_____

128. If you were an animal, what animal would you be?

_____

_____

_____

_____

_____

_____

_____

_____

129. If you were a color, what color would you be?

_____

_____

_____

_____

_____

_____

_____

_____

130. How are you feeling today, emotionally? Is this your usual state?

_____

_____

_____

_____

_____

_____

_____

_____

131. How are you feeling today, mentally? Is this your usual state?

_____

_____

_____

_____

_____

_____

_____

_____

132. How are you feeling today, physically? Is this your usual state?

_____

_____

_____

_____

_____

_____

_____

_____

133. How are you feeling today, spiritually? Is this your usual state?

_____

_____

_____

_____

_____

_____

_____

_____

134. What color would your emotional self be?

_____

_____

_____

_____

_____

_____

_____

135. What color would your mental self be?

_____

_____

_____

_____

_____

_____

_____

136. What color would your physical self be?

_____

_____

_____

_____

_____

_____

_____

137. What color would your spiritual self be?

_____

_____

_____

_____

_____

_____

_____

138. Do you feel you have a good relationship with your intuition?

_____

_____

_____

_____

_____

_____

_____

_____

139. Do you tend to listen more to your head or your heart?

_____

_____

_____

_____

_____

_____

_____

_____

140. When it comes to decision-making, do you tend to spend a lot of time thinking things through, or are you a "go with your gut" type of person?

_____

_____

_____

_____

_____

_____

_____

_____

141. In your opinion, what is your best asset?

_____

_____

_____

_____

_____

_____

_____

_____

142. Do you find it easy to define yourself with titles (occupation, profession, etc.) or challenging?

_____

_____

_____

_____

_____

_____

_____

_____

143. Do you find yourself wearing/having many different hats/titles?

_____

_____

_____

_____

_____

_____

_____

_____

144. What is your work-life balance like? Do you feel you have a good balance between work and home?

_____

_____

_____

_____

_____

_____

_____

_____

145. Do you feel you are good at setting boundaries?

_____

_____

_____

_____

_____

_____

_____

_____

146. How does your work personality differ from your home personality?

_____

_____

_____

_____

_____

_____

_____

_____

147. What do you do to unwind?

_____

_____

_____

_____

_____

_____

_____

_____

148. What brings you peace?

_____

_____

_____

_____

_____

_____

_____

_____

149. When do you feel most like yourself?

_____

_____

_____

_____

_____

_____

_____

_____

150. When do you feel most grounded?

_____

_____

_____

_____

_____

_____

_____

151. When do you feel most alive?

_____

_____

_____

_____

_____

_____

_____

Questions of The Future

WHERE ARE YOU GOING?

152. Is there anything in your life right now that you feel is holding you back?

_____

_____

_____

_____

_____

_____

_____

_____

153. Is there anything in your life right now you'd like to let go of?

_____

_____

_____

_____

_____

_____

_____

_____

154. What are the things in your life that are most important to you?

_____

_____

_____

_____

_____

_____

_____

_____

155. Do you feel that you actively give your energy where you want to be putting it?

_____

_____

_____

_____

_____

_____

_____

_____

156. In what ways would you like to grow?

_____

_____

_____

_____

_____

_____

_____

_____

157. Over the next six months, what are your intentions? Anything you'd like to overcome? Anything you'd like to prioritize or put more of your energy into?

_____

_____

_____

_____

_____

_____

_____

_____

158. Is there a specific goal you'd like to accomplish in the next six months?

_____

_____

_____

_____

_____

_____

_____ .

159. Six months from now, where do you think you'll be? What will you be doing? Will things be the same as now for you or quite different? What will change? What will be the same?

_____

_____

_____

_____

_____

_____

_____ .

160. What do you want to be doing in six to twelve months? What excites you about looking forward? How is what you want to be doing, different from what you think you'll be doing, in six months?

_____

_____

_____

_____

_____

_____

_____

_____

161. What steps do you need to take to move in that direction?

_____

_____

_____

_____

_____

_____

_____

162. Where do you see yourself in two years?

_____

_____

_____

_____

_____

_____

_____

_____.

163. Did you answer the last question, based on "being realistic" or "in a dream scenario"? What would your answer be if you took the other approach?

_____

_____

_____

_____

_____

_____

_____

_____.

164. What separates these different versions of your evolution? What limits you from living your dream scenario?

_____

_____

_____

_____

_____

_____

_____

_____

165. If you could ask a genie for three wishes, what would they be? (They can't be for more wishes because that's silly).

_____

_____

_____

_____

_____

_____

_____

_____

166. Could you bring any of these wishes to fruition for yourself?

_____

_____

_____

_____

_____

_____

_____

167. What is your deepest desire?

_____

_____

_____

_____

_____

_____

_____

_____

168. How would you describe your dream home?

_____

_____

_____

_____

_____

_____

_____

169. When you think of pure happiness, what comes to mind? Where are you? Who is with you? What are you doing?

_____

_____

_____

_____

_____

_____

_____

170. Are you currently designing your life in a way that aligns with this happiness you've just imagined? How or how not? What is one little thing you could do right now to bring 1% more happiness into your life?

_____

_____

_____

_____

_____

_____

_____

171. Did you choose your path in life, or was it thrust upon you?

_____

_____

_____

_____

_____

_____

_____

172. What is your primary goal? It can be personal or professional, internal or in relationships. Something you always come back to as your goal/intention.

_____

_____

_____

_____

_____

_____

_____

_____

173. Has this goal always been your goal, or has it changed over time?

_____

_____

_____

_____

_____

_____

_____

_____

174. What are the top five things on your bucket list?

_____

_____

_____

_____

_____

_____

_____

_____

175. If you could do any of these things tomorrow, which one would you pick? Why does this one come first?

_____

_____

_____

_____

_____

_____

_____

_____

176. If you don't have children, do you want children? If you do have children, did you always want children? How do you find you relate to children, whether your own or in general?

_____

_____

_____

_____

_____

_____

_____

_____

177. How does having/not having children change the direction you're headed in life? What would life be like if you were in the opposite situation?

_____

_____

_____

_____

_____

_____

_____

_____

178. What is something you've always wanted to do, yet never had the chance? What is stopping you, or has stopped you in the past, from doing that thing?

_____

_____

_____

_____

_____

_____

_____

179. Is there something you can do right now, to bring you closer to where you want to be?

_____

_____

_____

_____

_____

_____

_____

180. Where do you see yourself in five years?

_____

_____

_____

_____

_____

_____

_____

_____

181. Do you have a five-year plan? Do you feel you need a plan laid out, or do you prefer to flow through things as they come?

_____

_____

_____

_____

_____

_____

_____

_____

182. Do you find it easy to envision your future, or is it easier for you to not look too far ahead?

_____

_____

_____

_____

_____

_____

_____

_____.

183. What do you currently do to care for your future self? What, if anything, do you currently do that will provide a better quality of life for your future self? This could be as simple as wearing sunscreen or maintaining a professional accreditation.

_____

_____

_____

_____

_____

_____

_____

_____.

184. Thinking back for a moment, was there a time in your life when you envisioned your future self doing the things you're doing now? How does this reflection feel?

_____

_____

_____

_____

_____

_____

_____

_____

185. Have you always been on a very linear path, or has yours been a windy or rocky road? Do you most often find yourself on one or the other? What does this say about you?

_____

_____

_____

_____

_____

_____

_____

_____

186. What is one core value you will bring with you into the future?

_____

_____

_____

_____

_____

_____

_____

_____

_____

_____

_____

_____

_____

_____

_____

_____

Going Inward

187. Who are you when you're alone?

_____

_____

_____

_____

_____

_____

_____

188. Do you take time often to be with yourself?

_____

_____

_____

_____

_____

_____

_____

189. Do you find it easy, or challenging, to be alone?

_____

_____

_____

_____

_____

_____

_____

190. Do you consider yourself introverted or extroverted?

_____

_____

_____

_____

_____

_____

_____

191. How do you recharge? What are the things you can do to bring yourself back to your optimal state when you're tired, stressed, overwhelmed, etc.? What energizes you?

_____

_____

_____

_____

_____

_____

_____.

192. What do you consider your biggest weakness? Where does it come from?

_____

_____

_____

_____

_____

_____

_____.

193. Have you always been that way/carried this challenge?

_____

_____

_____

_____

_____

_____

_____

194. What is your greatest insecurity? Where does it come from?

_____

_____

_____

_____

_____

_____

_____

195. What is your relationship with your inner child like? What age are they? When do they most often come to the surface?

_____

_____

_____

_____

_____

_____

_____

_____

196. What does your inner child need?

_____

_____

_____

_____

_____

_____

_____

_____

197. What is your relationship with your "shadow" like? Your shadow is not necessarily a dark or scary part of you; it is the parts of you that you hide away from the world. You can refer to this as your "cringy" side, or your less filtered, less composed, self.

_____

_____

_____

_____

_____

_____

_____

_____

_____

198. What does your shadow self need?

_____

_____

_____

_____

_____

_____

_____

_____

199. What lives in your shadow and why was it banished here, instead of being allowed to live out in the world?

_____

_____

_____

_____

_____

_____

_____

_____

200. What does it sound like when you talk to yourself? Are you loving and kind to yourself? Are you judgemental? Are you angry? Are you resentful?

_____

_____

_____

_____

_____

_____

_____

_____

201. What do you worry about?

_____

_____

_____

_____

_____

_____

_____

_____

202. Do you find it easy, or challenging, to develop relationships?

_____

_____

_____

_____

_____

_____

_____

_____

203. What is the most challenging aspect of relationships for you? What types of relationships are most challenging? What scares you most about relationships?

_____

_____

_____

_____

_____

_____

_____

_____.

204. Do you find it challenging to speak your mind, or are you usually able to express yourself, in social situations? One-on-one? At work? With me?

_____

_____

_____

_____

_____

_____

_____

_____.

205. What scares you most about yourself?

_____

_____

_____

_____

_____

_____

_____

206. What scares you most about 'me'?

_____

_____

_____

_____

_____

_____

_____

207. Are you the type to hold a grudge?

_____

_____

_____

_____

_____

_____

_____

_____

208. How do you process your emotions? Do you have a particular practice or way of dealing with them?

_____

_____

_____

_____

_____

_____

_____

209. When do you feel most grounded?

_____

_____

_____

_____

_____

_____

_____

_____

210. Do you have any grounding practices you like to use? For example,

_____

_____

_____

_____

_____

_____

_____

211. What is your self-care routine like? Do you have a daily self-care ritual of some kind? A morning routine that makes you feel ready to take on the day? An evening routine that helps you relax and unwind?

_____

_____

_____

_____

_____

_____

212. How do you experience pleasure? How do you offer pleasure to yourself?

_____

_____

_____

_____

_____

_____

_____

213. Do you feel you are worthy of pleasure?

_____

_____

_____

_____

_____

_____

_____

214. Do you think you are a good person?

_____

_____

_____

_____

_____

_____

_____

215. Do you think others should love you?

_____

_____

_____

_____

_____

_____

_____

_____

216. Do you feel loved?

_____

_____

_____

_____

_____

_____

_____

_____

217. Do you love yourself?

_____

_____

_____

_____

_____

_____

_____

_____

_____

_____

_____

_____

_____

_____

_____

Going Outward

218. Do you consider yourself social?

_____

_____

_____

_____

_____

_____

_____

219. In what sort of spaces do you feel most like yourself?

_____

_____

_____

_____

_____

_____

_____

220. Do you prefer social situations to be one-on-one, or in bigger groups?

_____

_____

_____

_____

_____

_____

_____

_____ .

221. What do you feel is your biggest obstacle when making new friends?

_____

_____

_____

_____

_____

_____

_____

_____ .

222. Do you enjoy socializing with my friends?

_____

_____

_____

_____

_____

_____

_____

_____

223. What are others' first impressions of you, usually?

_____

_____

_____

_____

_____

_____

_____

_____

224. Do you identify with the way others perceive you?

_____

_____

_____

_____

_____

_____

_____

_____

225. Who in your life do you think sees you most clearly/understands you best?

_____

_____

_____

_____

_____

_____

_____

226. Do you ever struggle to feel seen?

_____

_____

_____

_____

_____

_____

_____.

227. Do you ever struggle to feel heard?

_____

_____

_____

_____

_____

_____

_____.

228. Do you consider yourself a good listener?

_____

_____

_____

_____

_____

_____

_____

_____

229. What does "active listening" mean to you?

_____

_____

_____

_____

_____

_____

_____

_____

230. Are you easily embarrassed? What is the most embarrassing experience you've ever had?

_____

_____

_____

_____

_____

_____

_____

231. Are you easily intimidated? Who, or what types of people, do you feel intimidated by?

_____

_____

_____

_____

_____

_____

_____

232. What is your ideal date? Describe a perfect date for me.

_____

_____

_____

_____

_____

_____

_____

_____

233. What time of year do you feel you're most social? Why do you think that is?

_____

_____

_____

_____

_____

_____

_____

_____

234. Do you enjoy special occasions/holidays/gatherings of this sort?

_____

_____

_____

_____

_____

_____

_____

_____

235. Are you particularly festive? Do you enjoy getting into the spirit of holidays?

_____

_____

_____

_____

_____

_____

_____

_____

236. At parties, are you usually the host, the life of the party, the helper, or the fly on the wall? Where do you usually fit in?

_____

_____

_____

_____

_____

_____

_____

_____.

237. Is your schedule usually completely packed full, or do you find yourself with lots of downtimes? Do you do this on purpose? Why?

_____

_____

_____

_____

_____

_____

_____

_____.

238. When do you feel most supported? What do you need to feel supported?

_____

_____

_____

_____

_____

_____

_____

_____

239. How can I support you better? Is there anything that I could do more, to make you feel more supported?

_____

_____

_____

_____

_____

_____

_____

_____

Reflections

240. Can you think of a time when someone advocated for you/stood up for you in a powerful way?

_____

_____

_____

_____

_____

_____

_____

_____

241. Can you think of a time when you advocated for/stood up for someone else in a powerful way?

_____

_____

_____

_____

_____

_____

_____

242. What is the primary trait you feel you've inherited from your mother or learned from other female role models in your life? Do you like this thing about yourself?

_____

_____

_____

_____

_____

_____

_____

_____.

243. What is the primary trait you feel you've inherited from your father or learned from other male role models in your life? Do you like this thing about yourself?

_____

_____

_____

_____

_____

_____

_____

_____.

244. Is there anything you feel you need to apologize for?

_____

_____

_____

_____

_____

_____

_____

_____

245. Is there anything you feel you deserve an apology for?

_____

_____

_____

_____

_____

_____

_____

_____

246. What is one thing you wish you had done differently? What would you have done differently? Why?

_____

_____

_____

_____

_____

_____

_____

247. How can you hold compassion for your younger self?

_____

_____

_____

_____

_____

_____

_____

248. How can you hold compassion for your present self?

_____

_____

_____

_____

_____

_____

_____

_____

249. Do you find you have a strong work ethic or are you more of a "meet the standards," bare minimum kind of person when it comes to projects, work, or things of this nature? Do you find it easy, or challenging, to self-motivate?

_____

_____

_____

_____

_____

_____

_____

_____

250. Why do you feel your work ethic is the way that it is?

_____

_____

_____

_____

_____

_____

_____

_____

251. What is your relationship to money? How has money played a role in your life?

_____

_____

_____

_____

_____

_____

_____

252. Do you consider yourself particularly self-aware?

_____

_____

_____

_____

_____

_____

_____

253. Are you good at taking risks?

_____

_____

_____

_____

_____

_____

_____

254. Are you good at being spontaneous, or do you need long-term plans?

_____

_____

_____

_____

_____

_____

_____

_____.

255. Are you detail-oriented, or big-picture-oriented?

_____

_____

_____

_____

_____

_____

_____

_____.

256. Are you usually the leader, or the follower?

_____

_____

_____

_____

_____

_____

_____

_____

257. What are the things, or who are the people, that cause you to reflect the most?

_____

_____

_____

_____

_____

_____

_____

_____

258. Do you enjoy looking in the mirror? Why or why not?

_____

_____

_____

_____

_____

_____

_____

259. How do you feel when you see your reflection?

_____

_____

_____

_____

_____

_____

_____

260. Who do you see when you see your reflection? Is there a particular person you resemble, even if it's just to yourself? What parts of yourself stand out to you, in the mirror? Do you like this or resent it? Or perhaps somewhere in the middle.

_____

_____

_____

_____

_____

_____

_____

261. Who in your life acts as a mirror to you (makes you see the things in yourself you wouldn't normally notice/see)? Do you appreciate this about this person, or do you find it challenging to handle?

_____

_____

_____

_____

_____

_____

_____

262. Thinking back for a moment, can you recall a time that a failure became a great lesson in your life? Tell me about it, how did failure redirect you to a lesson?

_____

_____

_____

_____

_____

_____

_____

_____.

263. Are you good at receiving criticism?

_____

_____

_____

_____

_____

_____

_____

_____.

264. What is the largest behavioral pattern you have overcome?

_____

_____

_____

_____

_____

_____

_____

_____

265. What has been the hardest thing for you to let go of in your life? Why?

_____

_____

_____

_____

_____

_____

_____

_____

266. What has been the greatest blessing in your life? Why?

_____

_____

_____

_____

_____

_____

_____

267. When do you feel most grateful?

_____

_____

_____

_____

_____

_____

_____

268. What are you grateful for?

_____

_____

_____

_____

_____

_____

_____

_____

_____

_____

_____

_____

_____

_____

_____

In Relation

269. Are you most commonly single, or in a relationship?

_____

_____

_____

_____

_____

_____

_____

_____

270. Does it often take you quite a while to get back into a new relationship after one ends? Or are you able to jump right into something new?

_____

_____

_____

_____

_____

_____

_____

_____

271. Do you find it natural to be in a romantic relationship?

_____

_____

_____

_____

_____

_____

_____

_____

272. What is your greatest challenge in developing relationships?

_____

_____

_____

_____

_____

_____

_____

_____

273. Do you find yourself more monogamous, or polyamorous?

_____

_____

_____

_____

_____

_____

_____

_____

274. What is your love language? (Your love language is how you need to experience love to feel loved. The five basic love languages are - physical touch, acts of service, gifts, words of affirmation, and quality time)

_____

_____

_____

_____

_____

_____

_____

_____

275. What is your definition of love? What does the word "love" mean to you? How do you experience love? How do you give love/show your love?

_____

_____

_____

_____

_____

_____

_____

_____.

276. Who in your life most influenced how you love?

_____

_____

_____

_____

_____

_____

_____

_____.

277. Do you consider yourself affectionate?

_____

_____

_____

_____

_____

_____

_____

278. What is your favorite thing about our relationship?

_____

_____

_____

_____

_____

_____

_____

279. How do I complement or balance you?

_____

_____

_____

_____

_____

_____

_____

280. Do you feel that I understand you?

_____

_____

_____

_____

_____

_____

_____

281. Are your relationships important to you? Or are you more of a lone wolf? How do you show this/enact this?

_____

_____

_____

_____

_____

_____

_____

_____

282. How do you prioritize your relationships?

_____

_____

_____

_____

_____

_____

_____

_____

283. What is your biggest strength when your loved ones need support? Are you able to support them? How do you do this? Are you the person people call when they need support?

_____

_____

_____

_____

_____

_____

_____

_____

284. Are there specific traits you look for in a partner? Why?

_____

_____

_____

_____

_____

_____

_____

_____

285. Have you noticed any negative patterns in how you choose your partners?

_____

_____

_____

_____

_____

_____

_____

_____

286. How have your parents/your upbringing influenced your choice of partners?

_____

_____

_____

_____

_____

_____

_____

_____

287. Do you find it easy to let people know you deeply?

_____

_____

_____

_____

_____

_____

_____

_____

288. Do you feel close to many people at once? Or do you have a select one or two people that know you deeply, and keep everyone else at a distance?

_____

_____

_____

_____

_____

_____

_____

_____

289. What is your relationship to vulnerability?

_____

_____

_____

_____

_____

_____

_____

290. What does intimacy mean to you?

_____

_____

_____

_____

_____

_____

_____

291. Do you feel safe being vulnerable with me?

_____

_____

_____

_____

_____

_____

_____

292. Do you find it easy to trust others?

_____

_____

_____

_____

_____

_____

_____

293. Are you naturally optimistic, or skeptical? Were you always this way? Which way are your parents?

_____

_____

_____

_____

_____

_____

_____

_____

294. Are you naturally glass half full, or half empty? Were you always this way? Which way are your parents or those that raised you?

_____

_____

_____

_____

_____

_____

_____

_____

295. What example of love and relationships did your family set during your childhood?

_____

_____

_____

_____

_____

_____

_____

_____

296. Do you believe in soulmates?

_____

_____

_____

_____

_____

_____

_____

_____

297. What does "soulmate" mean to you?

_____

_____

_____

_____

_____

_____

_____

_____

298. Do you find yourself often in conflict?

_____

_____

_____

_____

_____

_____

_____

_____

299. Do you consider yourself confrontational?

_____

_____

_____

_____

_____

_____

_____

300. How do you handle conflict?

_____

_____

_____

_____

_____

_____

_____

301. How do you heal from conflict?

_____

_____

_____

_____

_____

_____

_____

_____

302. How do you heal from heartbreak?

_____

_____

_____

_____

_____

_____

_____

_____

303. Who can you count on, no matter what?

_____

_____

_____

_____

_____

_____

_____

_____

304. Who would you call in the middle of the night to get you out of a jam?

_____

_____

_____

_____

_____

_____

_____

_____

305. Do you tend to maintain friendships for long periods, or are you always in and out of friendships and relationships? When the going gets tough, do you flee or fight?

_____

_____

_____

_____

_____

_____

_____

_____

306. Do you consider yourself good at maintaining long-distance friendships/relationships? Have you ever had to do this? Tell me about it.

_____

_____

_____

_____

_____

_____

_____

_____

307. Do you consider yourself good at recognizing when relationships (platonic or romantic) are unhealthy for you?

_____

_____

_____

_____

_____

_____

_____

_____.

308. What are some things you absolutely cannot tolerate in relationships (romantic/non-romantic)?

_____

_____

_____

_____

_____

_____

_____

_____.

309. What have you learned about yourself through your relationships?

_____

_____

_____

_____

_____

_____

_____

_____.

310. What is something that one of your relationships has changed your mind about?

_____

_____

_____

_____

_____

_____

_____

_____.

311. Can you think of a time that a relationship pushed you far outside of your comfort zone, for the best? What did you learn from this experience?

_____

_____

_____

_____

_____

_____

_____

_____

_____.

312. Can you think of a time that a relationship pushed you far outside of your comfort zone, for the worst? What did you learn from this experience?

_____

_____

_____

_____

_____

_____

_____

_____.

313. Can you think of a time you took a large risk, in a relationship? How did things pan out? Was it worth it?

_____

_____

_____

_____

_____

_____

_____

_____.

314. Do you feel confident sexually?

_____

_____

_____

_____

_____

_____

_____

_____.

315. If you could describe your sexual self in one word, what would it be?

_____

_____

_____

_____

_____

_____

_____

316. Do you feel you are open-minded sexually?

_____

_____

_____

_____

_____

_____

_____

317. What is your favorite thing about our sex life?

_____

_____

_____

_____

_____

_____

_____

_____

318. What is something you'd like to explore sexually?

_____

_____

_____

_____

_____

_____

_____

_____

319. What is the sexiest thing about me?

_____

_____

_____

_____

_____

_____

_____

320. What is your biggest turn-on?

_____

_____

_____

_____

_____

_____

_____

321. Do you have any kinks? Fetishes? Fantasies?

_____

_____

_____

_____

_____

_____

_____

_____.

322. Do you feel nervous during sex, or deeply relaxed?

_____

_____

_____

_____

_____

_____

_____

_____.

323. What have you learned about sex from past relationships?

_____

_____

_____

_____

_____

_____

_____

324. What have you learned about sex from our relationship?

_____

_____

_____

_____

_____

_____

_____

325. What is your biggest obstacle in sex?

_____

_____

_____

_____

_____

_____

_____

_____

326. When do you feel the sexiest?

_____

_____

_____

_____

_____

_____

_____

_____

327. When do you feel closest to me?

_____

_____

_____

_____

_____

_____

_____

_____

_____

_____

_____

_____

_____

_____

_____

This or That?

328. Chocolate or vanilla?

_____

_____

_____

_____

_____

_____

_____

329. Horror movie or a chick flick?

_____

_____

_____

_____

_____

_____

_____

330. Jeans or sweatpants?

_____

_____

_____

_____

_____

_____

_____

331. Burger and fries or a salad?

_____

_____

_____

_____

_____

_____

_____

332. Cats or dogs?

_____

_____

_____

_____

_____

_____

_____

_____

333. Inside or outside?

_____

_____

_____

_____

_____

_____

_____

_____

334. Five-mile hike or Netflix and chill?

_____

_____

_____

_____

_____

_____

_____

335. Big elaborate wedding or eloping?

_____

_____

_____

_____

_____

_____

_____

336. Beach day or winter sports?

_____

_____

_____

_____

_____

_____

_____

337. Beer or wine?

_____

_____

_____

_____

_____

_____

_____

338. Vodka or Whiskey?

_____

_____

_____

_____

_____

_____

_____

339. Country music or hip-hop?

_____

_____

_____

_____

_____

_____

_____

340. Rain or sunshine?

_____

_____

_____

_____

_____

_____

_____.

341. Vinyl record or Spotify?

_____

_____

_____

_____

_____

_____

_____.

342. Pick-up truck or luxury sports car?

_____

_____

_____

_____

_____

_____

_____

_____

343. Urban apartment or country home?

_____

_____

_____

_____

_____

_____

_____

_____

344. City streets or nature walk?

_____

_____

_____

_____

_____

_____

_____

345. Hot or cold?

_____

_____

_____

_____

_____

_____

_____

346. Night at the club or night in with a book?

_____

_____

_____

_____

_____

_____

_____

347. Disney or Marvel?

_____

_____

_____

_____

_____

_____

_____

348. Romance novel or comic book?

_____

_____

_____

_____

_____

_____

_____

349. Halloween or Christmas?

_____

_____

_____

_____

_____

_____

_____

350. Morning or evening?

_____

_____

_____

_____

_____

_____

_____

351. Coffee or tea?

_____

_____

_____

_____

_____

_____

_____

Couples Trivia

352. What is my favorite movie?

_____

_____

_____

_____

_____

_____

_____

353. What is my favorite snack?

_____

_____

_____

_____

_____

_____

_____

354. What is my favorite song?

_____

_____

_____

_____

_____

_____

_____

355. What is my middle name?

_____

_____

_____

_____

_____

_____

_____

356. What is the name of my hometown?

_____

_____

_____

_____

_____

_____

_____

_____

357. What was my first pet?

_____

_____

_____

_____

_____

_____

_____

_____

358. How would I spend my most perfect day?

_____

_____

_____

_____

_____

_____

_____

359. Where would I love to travel?

_____

_____

_____

_____

_____

_____

_____

360. What is my favorite sex position?

_____

_____

_____

_____

_____

_____

_____

361. What is my favorite outfit of yours?

_____

_____

_____

_____

_____

_____

_____

362. What is my favorite drink?

_____

_____

_____

_____

_____

_____

_____

363. What is my favorite animal?

_____

_____

_____

_____

_____

_____

_____

364. Am I a good dancer?

_____

_____

_____

_____

_____

_____

_____

_____

365. Am I a good singer?

_____

_____

_____

_____

_____

_____

_____

_____

366. How much do I love you?

_____

_____

_____

_____

_____

_____

_____

_____

_____

_____

_____

_____

_____

_____

_____

Conclusion

Hopefully, by now you've learned some things about one another that you never knew before. How do you feel? You most likely have had some surprises, some "ah-ha" moments, maybe some tears, and hopefully lots of laughs along this journey together. And maybe you feel closer to one another than you did before you opened this book. Are you feeling more compassion toward one another? Or are you feeling caught off guard?

Questions can be tricky. Sometimes we steer clear of them simply because we fear the answer we might receive. Sometimes we avoid them because we don't want the same question to be asked of us! Where does this fear come from? The invitation with this book is to release the fear, to be as honest as possible, and to perhaps learn not only about your partner but also maybe a little more about yourself. Maybe some things were quite challenging to answer, maybe some things caused you to consider something in a way you had never considered before. How did it feel to have your partner witness your striving to answer the challenging questions? Did you have patience with one another?

Keep these questions in your back pocket and see if you can integrate them - or simply the honesty that came with them - in other areas and other relationships in your life. Can you be more honest with your family? With your boss? With yourself? Can you find a way to get to know yourself a little better, each day of the year?

You have been brave, truth seekers - don't ever stop questioning!